MW01243489

TABLE OF CONTENTS

THE CONSTITUTION OF THE REFORMED CHURCH IN THE UNITED STATES

Table of Contents

PREAMBLE

For the maintenance of truth and order in the propagation of Christianity, in accordance with the Word of God, the Reformed Church in the United States ordains this Constitution to be its fundamental law for government, doctrine, worship and work, and declares the same to have binding authority on all its members, congregations and judicatories.

PART I
MEMBERS – CONGREGATIONS – OFFICES

SECTION 1

Members

ARTICLE 1. All baptized persons are members in the Church, under its care and subject to its government and discipline.

ARTICLE 2. Persons received into full communion with the Church by confirmation, profession of faith, certificate, or renewal of profession shall be regarded as communicant members. They shall be entitled to the rights and privileges of the Church and can be deprived of them only by due process of discipline.

ARTICLE 3. Those baptized in infancy shall be received into full communion with the Church by confirmation, and unbaptized adults by baptism and profession of faith. In both cases, they shall first receive proper instruction in the truths of the Gospel and give satisfactory evidence of faith in the Lord Jesus Christ.

ARTICLE 4. At the discretion of the Spiritual Council, members of other branches of the Christian Church, in good and regular standing, may be received into the membership of the Reformed Church by certificate of dismission. If, however, such certificate cannot be obtained, they may be received by a renewal of their profession of faith in Christ. This does not preclude the Spiritual Council from deciding in either case, before they are thus received, whether or not they shall be instructed in the fundamental truths of the Christian religion as set forth in the Heidelberg Catechism, Belgic Confession and Canons of Dort.

ARTICLE 5. Members who have permanently changed their residence shall be urged by the minister or Spiritual Council to obtain a certificate of dismission and, as soon as possible, shall unite with another congregation of the Reformed Church, or another orthodox Protestant Church, as provided in ARTICLE 74. Members who for proper reasons, desire to unite with another congregation shall also be entitled to a certificate of dismission. The Spiritual Council dismissing members shall immediately communicate the fact to the Spiritual Council of the congregation to which they have been dismissed; and when they are received the latter shall promptly notify the former of their reception. Members dismissed shall be amenable to the congregation dismissing them until they have been received by the other congregation. A certificate of dismission shall be valid for one year from its date.

ARTICLE 6. It is the duty of Church members to live sober, righteous and godly lives, and to labor faithfully to bring others to Christ. They shall obey the laws and rules of life prescribed in the Word of God and abide by the Constitution of the Church and contribute liberally, in proportion to their means, to the support of the Gospel and for the extension of the Kingdom of Christ. Every member shall attend faithfully the public services of the Church and shall engage diligently in private devotions; and those who have been confirmed shall partake regularly of the Lord's Supper. Parents shall give attention to the Christian training of the members of the household.

SECTION 2

Congregations

ARTICLE 7. A congregation of the Reformed Church in the United States is a body of Christians accepting the Bible as the Word of God and the Heidelberg Catechism, the Belgic Confession of Faith, and the Canons of Dort as its subordinate standards of faith and doctrine, and organized agreeably to the provisions of the Constitution of the Church.

ARTICLE 8. Whenever it is desired to organize a congregation, those persons who are willing to enter into such organization shall sign the following memorial and address the same to the Classis within whose bounds the congregation is to be organized:

"We, whose names are hereunto affixed, desiring to be organized as a congregation, that we may have better facilities for enjoying the holy ordinances of the Christian Church, do hereby petition the Classis of _____ to organize us under the name of _____ congregation, in the township (town, or city) of _____, county of _____, and State of _____ and declare our readiness to be governed by the Constitution of the Reformed Church in the United States."

4

Date:_____

Signed: _____

If the Classis approves of the proposed organization, it shall appoint a committee to superintend the election of elders and deacons, and to induct them into office. After the acts thus authorized have been performed and have been sanctioned by the Classis, the organization shall be enrolled as a regular congregation of the Reformed Church in the United States. If, however, local conditions require it, a congregation may be duly organized by a missionary, or a minister doing missionary work, acting with the consent of the Classis under whose jurisdiction the congregation is to be received. Application for admission to Classis must be made as soon as possible after the organization is effected.

A congregation, whether independent or belonging to another denomination, which conforms to the requirements of the Reformed Church in the United States, may be admitted to membership.

ARTICLE 9. Whenever a congregation desires to become an incorporated body, a draft of the proposed Articles of Incorporation and Constitution of the congregation shall be submitted to the Classis for approval before the charter is presented to the civil authorities. A charter shall not be approved that does not bind the congregation to be an organic member of the Reformed Church in the United States, and to be governed by its Constitution and laws. In all cases, unless there are difficulties, the Consistory shall in the charter be constituted the trustees of the congregation.

ARTICLE 10. Each congregation shall adopt a Constitution and By-laws for its own government. Such Constitution and By-laws must be in accordance with its charter and with the Constitution of the Reformed Church in the United States; and must be approved by its Classis.

ARTICLE 11. Each congregation shall hold an annual meeting. The Consistory may call a special meeting of the congregation, and, at the written request of one-tenth of the communicant members, shall issue a call for such a meeting within two weeks after the request has been received. Two weeks previous public notice shall be given of the time, place, and the purpose of a special congregational meeting. A full and accurate record of the proceedings of all meetings shall be kept.

ARTICLE 12. To the trustees shall be committed the care and control of the property of the congregation, whether real or personal, and of all monies and legacies. They shall hold the property as a sacred trust for the congregation, keep the church edifice and other buildings belonging to the congregation in proper repair, and prevent their use for improper purposes. In matters of a general nature, such as the purchasing or selling of property, the borrowing of money, and the remodeling or erection of buildings, the trustees can determine nothing finally without the consent of a majority of those voting members of the congregation assembled at a meeting called for the purpose, of which meeting at least two weeks previous public notice shall be given.

ARTICLE 13. The common interests of two or more congregations united in one pastoral charge shall be committed to a Joint Consistory, composed of the members of the Consistories of the congregations included in the charge. A congregation shall not withdraw from such a charge without the permission of Classis.

ARTICLE 14. On the dissolution of a congregation, the Classis with which it was connected shall have jurisdiction over its members and transfer them to the congregation which they may select.

SECTION 3

Offices

ARTICLE 15. The Offices of the Reformed Church.

1. The Offices are:

    I.   The Office of Minister of the Word.

        a.   Students for the Ministry.

        b.   Licentiates.

        c.   Ministers of the Word.

        d.   Teachers of Theology.

    II.   The Office of Elder.

    III. The Office of Deacon.

2. The officers of the Reformed Church are to be male members who have the Biblical qualifications for office.

I. The Office of the Minister of the Word

1. Students for the Ministry

ARTICLE 16. A student for the ministry is a member of a congregation of the Reformed Church in the United States who, believing himself called to become a minister of Christ, enters upon a course of study to prepare himself for that office.

ARTICLE 17. A student for the ministry shall request that he be taken under the care of the Classis to which the congregation of which he is a member belongs. When he presents the request to be received, the Classis shall inquire as to his fitness and, if he is found satisfactory, shall take him under its care and exercise supervision over his studies and deportment. He shall pursue his course of study in a theological institution recommended by the Reformed Church in the United States, unless Classis permits him to study elsewhere. This permission can be given only if it does not conflict with any previous obligation he may have assumed.

ARTICLE 18. At each annual meeting of his Classis a student for the ministry shall submit a written report of the progress he has made in his studies, and also his official reports from the institution in which he is studying. He shall not exercise ministerial functions, but may occasionally preach after his first year in the Seminary.

A student for the ministry shall not be eligible to the pastoral office, nor shall a congregation or charge nominate or elect a student for the ministry to become its pastor until the latter half of the senior year of this theological course, when a charge may tender and a student accept a call which, however, shall not be confirmed by a Classis, nor become effective, until after his licensure.

2. Licentiates

ARTICLE 19. A licentiate is a member of the Reformed Church who, having completed a prescribed course of theological studies and having passed a satisfactory examination by a Classis, has been authorized to preach the Gospel and to accept a call from a pastoral charge or a missionary field.

ARTICLE 20. An applicant for licensure shall present a written application to his Classis, together with his certificate from the Theological Seminary or Institution in which he studied. He shall submit to an examination, which shall be open to all the members of Classis and shall embrace at least the main subjects taught in the Theological Seminaries approved by the Reformed Church in the United States. Particular attention shall be paid to his piety, the purity of his intentions in seeking the ministry, his orthodoxy, and his ability to preach the Gospel. The report of such examination shall not enter into particulars, but simply state the result as satisfactory or unsatisfactory.

The candidate is to show that he is not a weak and ignorant man. Therefore, he is to be examined by the Classis in English Bible, theology, ecclesiastical history, hermeneutics, the original languages of the Scriptures, historical philosophy, apologetics, all matters relevant to our standards and his personal ability to serve the Church as a pastor. The examination in theology must be on the floor of Classis and may not be a closed meeting but rather an open meeting of the Classis. He is also required to preach a sermon before Classis, present theological papers and present a written sermon.

ARTICLE 21. For good reasons licensure may be granted to applicants who have not completed the course of study prescribed for the Theological Seminaries, but in all such cases, a two-thirds vote of the Classis shall be required to authorize the licensure.

ARTICLE 22. After the examination of the applicant has been declared satisfactory and the report of the examiners has been adopted, he shall read aloud before Classis the following formula and subscribe the same in a book kept for that purpose:

"I hereby testify that I honestly and truly accept the doctrine of the Heidelberg Catechism, the Belgic Confession of Faith, and the Canons of Dort as in accordance with the teaching of the Holy Scriptures, and promise faithfully to preach and defend the same. I also declare and promise that I will carefully observe all the ordinances in accordance with the Word of God which now are, or may hereafter be enacted by the authorities of the Church, and that I will cheerfully submit to all the admonitions and decisions of these authorities so long as I remain in connection with the Reformed Church in the United States.

"In testimony whereof I hereunto subscribe my name and the date."

Name _____

Date _____

Having thus attested his adherence to the doctrines and discipline of the Reformed Church in the United States, he shall be furnished with a certificate of licensure, bearing the seal of Classis and the signatures of the President and Stated Clerk; and his name shall be placed on the clerical roll.

ARTICLE 23. A licentiate is permitted to preach the Word, but shall not administer the sacraments, pronounce the salutation, nor pronounce the benediction, neither shall he perform the rite of confirmation, participate in ordination, nor solemnize marriage. He is under the care and jurisdiction of his Classis, must attend its meetings and submit a written report of his labors, but he cannot vote in Classis nor can he represent it in a higher judicatory.

ARTICLE 24. A licentiate shall not be ordained before he is twenty-one years of age, and until he has received and accepted a call to a pastoral charge, or has been called to a mission or to be a Teacher of Theology in an authorized theological institution approved by the Reformed Church in the United States. A licentiate who has received and accepted a call from a pastoral charge shall be ordained either by the Classis within whose bounds the charge is located or by the Classis to which he belongs when accepting the call. A licentiate who has received and accepted a call to teach theology or to the presidency of an accredited educational institution approved by the Reformed Church, or to a chaplaincy in the army or navy of the United States of America, shall be ordained by the Classis to which he belongs when he accepts the call.

Before a licentiate is ordained to the Gospel ministry, he shall undergo trials. Trials for ordination for a candidate who has been licensed by the Classis shall consist of the following: (1) the evaluation of written and oral testimonials as to the candidate's satisfactory exercise of the gifts for the Gospel ministry; (2) an examination of any areas of weakness as evidenced in the candidate's licensure examination; (3) an examination, as the Classis may require, in the Confession and Constitution of the Church and the presentation of written discourses. If one-third of those voting in the Classis are dissatisfied with the examination, the candidate shall not be ordained but be required to undergo another examination at a future meeting of the Classis. A satisfactory vote of the majority on the second examination shall be sufficient for ordination. The report of the committee examining the candidate may report weaknesses and require further study in the weak areas. His progress is to be reported in his parochial report.

ARTICLE 25. A licentiate shall not preach statedly for a vacant congregation or pastoral charge without the consent of Classis. He shall be a member of that Classis within whose bounds he resides, except as provided for in the case of ministers in Article 31 of this Constitution.

ARTICLE 26. Before licentiates from another denomination can be received into a Classis of the Reformed Church in the United States, they shall be examined in the same manner as students are examined for licensure and ordination according to Articles 20 and 24, and shall subscribe the formula prescribed for licentiates. A licentiate from another denomination shall not be a candidate for a pastoral charge until he has received approval from Classis or a committee appointed by Classis, nor shall he receive a call from a charge until said call shall have been approved by Classis.

3. Ministers of the Word

ARTICLE 27. A Minister of the Word is a member of the Church, called by Christ to the ministry of reconciliation, and ordained and consecrated by prayer and the laying on of hands to preach the Gospel, to exercise pastoral oversight, to dispense the holy sacraments, in conjunction with the elders to administer Christian discipline, and to give himself wholly to the service of Christ in His Church.

ARTICLE 28. A minister of the Reformed Church in the United States receiving a call from a charge and accepting the same shall present said call together with his acceptance of it to Classis for consideration; and if the call is confirmed, provision shall be made at once for his installation as pastor. A call, however, shall not be confirmed unless it provides for adequate support of the pastor, and unless the salary of the preceding pastor shall have been paid or satisfactory arrangements for its payment have been made; nor shall any Classis refuse to confirm a call unless there are strong reasons for withholding such confirmation. A minister having received a call from a charge shall not move into it, without first having obtained the consent of Classis. Every pastor shall reside within the bounds of his charge, unless Classis gives him permission to reside elsewhere.

ARTICLE 29. Every pastor or secretary of the Consistory shall keep a complete record of all baptisms, confirmations, communicants, receptions by certificate, renewals of profession, dismissions, erasures of names, suspensions, excommunications, marriages and deaths. The record shall be the property of the congregation.

ARTICLE 30. A pastor desiring to resign his charge shall lay his resignation before the Consistory or Joint Consistory, which shall take action on it as soon as possible; but if the pastor or Consistory desires it, the resignation shall be laid before the congregation or congregations for action. The resignation, and the consequent action of the Consistory, or of the congregation or congregations, shall then as soon as possible be laid before the Classis for action. When in the opinion of three-fourths of the members of the Consistory of Joint Consistory the welfare of the charge requires it, the Consistory or Joint Consistory shall make a written request to the pastor for his resignation. If the pastor, or the Consistory or Joint Consistory, desires it, the request shall be laid before the congregation or congregations for action. If the majority of the congregation or congregations sustain the request, the matter shall then as soon as possible be referred to Classis for action. But if the request is not brought before the congregation or congregations, the matter shall be referred directly to the Classis. A pastor shall not leave his charge before his resignation has been approved and the pastoral relation has been dissolved by Classis.

ARTICLE 31. A minister shall not officiate in the charge of another minister without his consent; nor shall he serve a vacant congregation or charge as a regular supply without the consent of the Classis to which the congregation or charge belongs. He shall be a member of the Classis within whose bounds he resides, unless he shall have retired from the active duties of the ministry; or unless he is connected with an Institution of the Church, in which case he may be a member of any Classis connected with the Synod under whose care or by whose authority the Institution acts.

ARTICLE 32. A minister shall continue in the service of the Church. Direct denominational work shall be regarded as service to the Church. A minister of Classis shall not remain on the roll of Classis for more than three consecutive years without being engaged in the service of the Church. This article is not applicable to retired or disabled ministers.

ARTICLE 33. If a minister not otherwise chargeable with an offense renounces the jurisdiction of the Reformed Church in the United States by joining another denomination without being regularly dismissed to it, Classis shall record the fact and erase his name from the roll. If charges are pending against him, he may be tried on them. If the minister against whom the charges are pending shall have abandoned the ministry or declared himself independent, his name shall be erased, or he shall be deposed or excommunicated, as the case may require.

ARTICLE 34. A minister compelled by age or infirmity to retire from the active duties of the ministry shall retain his right to a seat and vote in his Classis and in the Synod, and to perform ministerial acts within the restrictions specified in Article 31 of this Constitution.

When any minister shall resign his charge by reason of age or incapacity for further labor, and the congregation shall be moved by affectionate regard for his person and gratitude for his ministry among them, to desire that he should continue to be associated with them in an honorary relation, they may, at a regularly called meeting, elect him as Pastor Emeritus, with or without salary, but with no pastoral authority or duty. This action shall be subject to the approval of Classis, and shall take effect upon the formal dissolution of the pastoral relation.

If the retiring minister lacks the means of self-support his Classis shall report his name to the Standing Committee on Ministerial Aid.

ARTICLE 35. A minister from another denomination, before he shall be admitted into the ministry of the Reformed Church in the United States, shall present a certificate of dismission, and shall be examined as to his orthodoxy and the purity of his intentions. If his application is approved, he shall upon signing the formula prescribed for licentiates, be admitted by a two-thirds vote of the Classis to which he has applied for reception. A minister from another denomination shall not be a candidate for a pastoral charge until he has received approval from Classis or a committee appointed by Classis, nor shall he receive a call from a charge until said call shall have been approved by Classis.

4. Teachers of Theology

ARTICLE 36. A Teacher of Theology is a Minister of the Word who has been elected and inaugurated as a professor in a Theological Seminary of the Church. He shall be chosen in such manner as may be determined by the Synod.

ARTICLE 37. A person shall not be elected a Teacher of Theology whose views are not in accord with the faith and doctrines of the Reformed Church in the United States and who does not approve of its mode of government, forms of worship and distinctive customs.

ARTICLE 38. Before a Teacher of Theology enters upon the duties of his office, he shall be inaugurated under the direction of the Synod. At his inauguration, he shall solemnly affirm the following declaration in a public assembly:

"—You _____, Professor-elect of the Theological Seminary of the Reformed Church in the United States, at_____, acknowledge sincerely before God and this assembly that the Holy Scriptures of the Old and New Testaments, which are called canonical, are divinely inspired Scriptures and therefore credible and authoritative; that they contain all things which relate to the faith, the practice and the hope of the righteous, and are the only rule of faith and practice in the Church of God; that, consequently, traditions, as they are called, and mere conclusions of reason that are contrary to the clear testimony of these Scriptures cannot be received as rules of faith or of life. You acknowledge, further, that the doctrine contained in the Heidelberg Catechism, the Belgic Confession of Faith, and the Canons of Dort is in accordance with the teaching of the Holy Scriptures. You declare sincerely, that in the office you are about to assume you will make the divine authority of the Holy Scriptures the basis of all your instructions, and faithfully maintain and defend the same. You declare, finally, that according to the ability which God may grant you, you will so labor that, with the divine blessing, the students entrusted to your care may become enlightened, pious, faithful and zealous ministers of the Gospel, who shall be sound in the faith." The Professor-elect shall answer, "—I so declare and affirm."

ARTICLE 39. Teachers of Theology shall explain the Holy Scriptures and defend the pure doctrine of the Gospel against errors. In their instructions to the theological students, it shall be their principal aim to make them well acquainted with the true sense of the Holy Scriptures, and prepare them to preach the Gospel with power and effect. In this service, they are required to instruct the students in Exegetical, Historical, Systematic and Practical Theology.

ARTICLE 40. A Teacher of Theology shall continue in office during his life, unless he resigns or becomes disqualified for his duties by heterodoxy or immorality, or by physical or mental infirmities.

ARTICLE 41. If two ministers and two elders of the Church, representing two different Classes, present to the Board of Visitors of any Theological Seminary a document asserting that, for cause or causes named in Article 40 of this Constitution, a Teacher of Theology is disqualified for his position, said Board shall institute a careful examination, and if the charge is well founded shall refer the matter for final disposition to the Synod. In all things except his position as Teacher of Theology, he is amenable to the Classis to which he belongs.

ARTICLE 42. A Teacher of Theology who has been rendered incapable of further service by infirmities shall not be displaced without having such provision made for his support as his necessities may require and as the Synod may be able to make. After the age of seventy, he shall be declared Professor Emeritus. A Teacher of Theology desiring to resign his office shall, at least six months before his resignation is to take effect, give notice in writing of his intention to the proper officers.

II. The Office of Elder

ARTICLE 43. An elder is a member of the Church chosen by a congregation and ordained to his office by prayer and the laying on of hands to assist and support the pastor in the spiritual affairs of the Church.

ARTICLE 44. Elders shall take heed to themselves that they be an example unto others, shall watch faithfully over the spiritual interests of the congregation, shall maintain order in the house of God, shall aid in visiting the sick and in family visitation, and shall contribute according to their ability to the edification and consolation of all members. They shall provide the elements for the Lord's Supper and aid in their distribution, when requested by the pastor or by the Spiritual Council.

III. The Office of Deacon

ARTICLE 45. A deacon is a member of the Church chosen by the congregation and ordained to office by prayer and the laying on of hands to aid in securing the funds necessary for the support of the Church in its various activities, and to foster the principles of stewardship, thereby cultivating the spirit of liberality and cheerful giving. He is to attend to the temporal affairs of the congregation, except such as are specified in Article 12 of this Constitution, and to look after the poor and needy in properly dispensing the charity of the Church.

ARTICLE 46. Elders and deacons shall be elected by a majority of the votes cast at a congregational meeting. Their number in the congregation, the question of their re-election and their term of office shall be determined by the Constitution and By-laws of the congregation. If possible, each congregation shall have at least two elders and two deacons. When elected for the first time they shall be publicly ordained to their office. After their ordination, they, with those who have been re-elected, shall be installed. Unless dismissed to another congregation they shall remain in office until their successors are inducted into office.

ARTICLE 47. Members called to the office of elder or deacon shall be of exemplary life and conduct (see Acts 6:1œ6 and 1 Tim. 3:8œ13), that the congregation may be edified. On this account light-minded, contentious, or otherwise improper persons shall not be chosen to these offices.

ARTICLE 48. Nominations for the offices of elder and deacon shall be made by the Consistory, which shall present the names of one or two persons for each officer to be elected. Public notice of the nominations shall be given from the pulpit at least one week before the election. On or before the meeting for the election one additional person for each officer to be elected may be nominated by the congregation. A person shall not be voted for unless regularly nominated. All nominees must be in full communion with the Church and earnestly devoted to the cause of Christ.

PART II JUDICATORIES

SECTION 1

Judicatories in General

ARTICLE 49. Judicatories, as used in this Constitution, may refer to a Consistory in reference to non-judicial actions, and to the Spiritual Council, Classis, and Synod in both judicial and non-judicial actions.

The judicatories are:

1. The Consistory.

2. The Spiritual Council.

3. The Classis.

4. The Synod.

They take cognizance only of ecclesiastical matters, and have authority to require obedience to the laws of Christ and His Church and to discipline the disobedient. Consistories do not adjudicate or have a judicial capacity. Only the Spiritual Council, Classis, and Synod adjudicate in disciplinary and doctrinal matters.

ARTICLE 50. Cases over which a lower judicatory has original jurisdiction can be brought before a higher judicatory only by reference, complaint or appeal.

ARTICLE 51. From the regular credentials of the delegates, primarii and secundi, the Stated Clerk of a Classis and the Synod shall prepare the roll in advance of the stated meeting. Irregular or disputed credentials shall be referred, immediately after the organization of the Judicatory, to a special committee, which shall report within twenty-four hours after its appointment. The sessions of every judicatory shall be opened and closed with religious services.

ARTICLE 52. A Classis and the Synod shall elect a President, a Stated Clerk, and such other officers as they may respectively deem necessary, who shall hold their offices for such term as the respective judicatories may determine.

ARTICLE 53. When a judicatory meets as a delegated body, the delegates to it shall be elected by the judicatories which they respectively represent from among their members, and in all such elections at least a double number of persons shall be nominated. Tellers shall be appointed to distribute, collect and count the ballots, and shall report the number of votes cast for any member to the President, who shall then declare the result. Those having the highest number of votes shall be the primarii, and an equal number having the next highest number of votes shall be the secundi, who shall succeed the primarii in the order of the number of votes received in both cases. In case delegates have received an equal number of votes, their names shall be arranged on the list in alphabetical order.

ARTICLE 54. Active elders only shall be ordinarily elected to judicatories. For good reasons, other elders may be seated by a two-thirds vote of the judicatory to which they have been elected. Elders shall have the same rights and privileges in a judicatory as Ministers of the Word.

ARTICLE 55. Delegates to a judicatory shall be punctual in attending its meetings and shall remain during the whole of its sessions. They are amenable for their tardiness or absence to the judicatory which elected them, which also must provide for the expenses incurred in attending to their duties unless paid by the higher judicatory.

ARTICLE 56. At a special meeting of a judicatory action can be taken only on the items of business specified in the call.

ARTICLE 57. If unforeseen circumstances should render it necessary, either the time or the place, or both, of the stated meeting of a Classis and the Synod may be changed by the President and Stated Clerk; provided that for a Classis two weeks and for the Synod four weeks previous notice is given by the President and Stated Clerk through a circular addressed to each member of the judicatory.

ARTICLE 58. At least one member of every committee appointed by Classis or the Synod shall be an elder.

ARTICLE 59. Delegates from bodies in correspondence with the Synod shall be recognized as advisory members, but they shall not have a vote. The same privilege shall be accorded to every minister and elder of the Reformed Church who, though not a delegate, is present at a meeting of the judicatory. Ministers from other denominations who are in attendance shall be recognized and welcomed by the President, but shall not be admitted to seats as advisory members.

ARTICLE 60. A member of a judicatory shall not be allowed to enter a protest against its acts; but any member dissenting shall have the right to call for the yeas and nays, in which case the vote and name of every member voting on the question shall be entered on the minutes, or any member may have his affirmative or negative vote recorded in the minutes.

SECTION 2

The Consistory

ARTICLE 61. The Consistory is composed of the pastor or pastors and the elders and deacons, and has oversight and government of the congregation and of all its organizations.

ARTICLE 62. The pastor shall be President of the Consistory, unless the existing charter provides otherwise. When a charge is without a pastor, or the pastor is unable to attend, one of the elders shall be chosen to preside. A majority of the members shall constitute a quorum, unless otherwise provided in the charter or constitution of the congregation.

ARTICLE 63. The Joint Consistory, as provided in Article 13 of this Constitution, is composed of the members of the Consistories included in the charge. It has jurisdiction over the common interests of the congregations represented, such as the calling of a pastor, the provision for his salary, and the erection and maintenance of a parsonage for the charge. The pastor shall be President; in the event of his absence or inability to preside, one of the elders may be chosen to preside.

ARTICLE 64. The Consistory shall hold stated monthly or quarterly meetings, and may hold such special meetings as are called by the President, or, in the event of his absence, or inability or unwillingness to act, by the Secretary when requested to do so by a majority of the members. Previous notice of special meetings of the Consistory or Joint Consistory shall be given to its members.

ARTICLE 65. The Consistory or the Joint Consistory shall annually elect delegates, a primarius and a secundus, to represent the charge in Classis, who shall also be the delegates to Synod whenever Synod meets in general convention. At least ten days before the annual meeting of the judicatory to which these delegates have been elected, their credentials shall be sent to its Stated Clerk by the President or the Secretary of the Consistory. Within ninety days after the annual meeting of the Classis, the Consistory or Joint Consistory shall meet and act upon all matters referred to it by the Classis, and immediately thereafter said action shall be reported to the Stated Clerk of Classis.

ARTICLE 66. In managing the general affairs of the congregation the

Consistory shall call congregational meetings, order collections for the apportionments of Classis and for other benevolent purposes, distribute alms through the deacons, provide for the audit of the treasurer's account, and make due provision for the support of the pastor. It shall keep a full an accurate record of its own proceedings, be the custodian of all congregational records, and submit any or all records to the Classis when occasion requires it and the Classis requests it.

ARTICLE 67. In all matters of a general nature, as specified in Article 12 of the Constitution, including the calling of a minister, the Consistory shall determine nothing conclusively without the consent of a majority of those voting members of the congregation present at a meeting duly called for the purpose, of which at least two weeks public notice shall be given.

ARTICLE 68. In the election of a minister, the Consistory or Joint Consistory shall, as soon as possible, present to the congregation or congregations constituting the charge, the name of one candidate for the pastorate, to be voted upon at a meeting called for the purpose, of which public notice shall be given at least two weeks previously. The voting members shall vote by ballot for or against the candidate. He is elected if a majority of the members of the charge present and voting cast their vote in his favor, unless a larger portion is required by the charter. The Consistory or Joint Consistory shall then tender him a call according to the form prescribed by the Synod. If a pastoral charge consists of two or more congregations, the election shall be held, if possible, in each Congregation on the same day. The ballots cast by each congregation shall be sealed, and when all the congregations have voted a committee of tellers, appointed by the Joint Consistory, shall count the ballots as the vote of the charge. In no circumstances shall a congregation or charge vote on more than one candidate at one and the same meeting.

ARTICLE 69. When a charge is without a pastor the Consistory or Joint Consistory shall invite the Executive Committee of Classis or the officers of Classis to consult with them, and assist them in filling the vacancy and to make provision for the temporary supply of the pulpit. This consultation shall be held within a month after the pulpit has been declared vacant by Classis.

The supply shall be either a minister, a licentiate, or a student for the ministry of the Reformed Church in the United States, in good and regular standing. In exceptional cases, at the discretion of Classis, permission to supply a vacant charge may be granted to a duly qualified minister of another denomination. A temporary supply shall not continue longer than one year unless by action of Classis.

SECTION 3

The Spiritual Council

ARTICLE 70. The Spiritual Council consists of the pastor or pastors and the active elders of a congregation. It has original jurisdiction in matters of discipline except in the case of a Minister of the Word.

ARTICLE 71. The pastor shall be President of the Spiritual Council; if the congregation is without a pastor, one of the elders shall be chosen to preside. A majority of its members shall constitute a quorum.

ARTICLE 72. It is the duty of the Spiritual Council to watch over the members of the congregation, to guard the doctrine of Christ, and to maintain wholesome discipline. It alone has the power to admit members to full communion and to exclude any who may err from the faith or offend in morals.

ARTICLE 73. Stated meetings of the Spiritual Council shall be held for the examination of the catechumens applying for confirmation. Special meetings shall be held at the call of the President or at the request of two elders.

ARTICLE 74. The Spiritual Council shall, at its discretion and upon proper request, furnish members of the congregation, in good and regular standing, with certificates of dismission to another congregation in the Reformed Church or to any orthodox Protestant Church which receives members by certificate from the Reformed Church in the United States. The certificate shall specify the congregation to which the person is dismissed.

ARTICLE 75. The Spiritual Council shall keep a full and accurate record of its proceedings, which shall be submitted to the Classis when occasion requires it and the Classis requests it.

SECTION 4

The Classis

ARTICLE 76. A Classis consists of the ministers residing within a district designated by the Synod and of the elders delegated by the pastoral charges situated within these limits, and has jurisdiction over said ministers and pastoral charges.

ARTICLE 77. A Classis shall embrace at least three pastoral charges and as many ordained ministers. It shall meet regularly in the spring and may also meet regularly in the fall each year at such time and place as it may designate. Three ministers and two delegated elders regularly convened shall constitute a quorum.

ARTICLE 78. Each pastoral charge shall be represented in Classis by its pastor or pastors and one delegated elder; or, if the charge is without a pastor, by a delegated elder.

ARTICLE 79. The annual meeting of a Classis shall be opened with religious services, including the preaching of a sermon by the President, or by one of its members designated by him or by the Classis, after which the roll shall be called; if a quorum is present, the officers for the ensuing year shall be elected, and the business shall proceed according to the Rules of Order prescribed by the Synod.

ARTICLE 80. The President shall perform all the duties of his office as defined by the Rules of Order. Immediately after the election of officers, he shall define the Bar of the House, and appoint the Standing Committees of Classis, which shall present their reports as soon as possible. The reports of the Committees on Minutes of Classis, Minutes of Synod, and on Overtures shall exhibit those items which claim the attention of the Classis.

ARTICLE 81. At the spring meeting every pastor shall present a written parochial and full statistical report, and every minister, though without a charge, a report of his labors. If unable to be present, he shall forward his report to the Stated Clerk three days before the meeting. The parochial report shall contain a full account of the spiritual and temporal condition of the charge and of the labors of the pastor, the President or any member of the Classis shall ask the pastor and the elder such questions as may be requisite to elicit additional information. The President shall then address the following questions to each elder:

1. Are the doctrines of the Gospel preached in your charge in their purity, agreeably to the Word of God?

2. Is careful attention given to the instruction of the youth for confirmation, the reception of members into the Church, and the Christian nurture of the members?

3. In providing spiritual nurture for the congregation:

    a. Is visitation faithfully performed?

b. Is Christian discipline faithfully exercised according to the Constitution?

4. Are the sacraments of Holy Baptism and the Lord's Supper properly administered in accordance with the Constitution?

5. In providing for the furtherance of Christian stewardship:

   a. Are the apportionments for the Classis paid according to the Guidelines for Giving?

   b. Are these monies sent promptly to the Classis treasurer?

   c. Are the apportionments for the Synod paid according to the Guidelines for Giving?

   d. Are these monies sent promptly to the Synod treasurer?

6. Are the Church records properly kept?

7a. Is the temporal contract between minister and people fulfilled in your charge?

7b. Is the temporal contract between minister and people adequate to meet his temporal needs?

The Statistical Report shall be prepared according to the form approved by the Synod. If a charge is without a pastor, the Consistory or Joint Consistory shall furnish the parochial and statistical reports. The President of the Executive Committee of Classis shall annually submit a report to the Classis on the state of the Church, making use of the parochial reports.

At the fall meeting the Classis shall give special attention to the work of the denomination.

ARTICLE 82. In every Classis is vested the power to examine and license applicants for the ministry, to ordain licentiates, to constitute or dissolve pastoral relations, to receive and dismiss ministers and licentiates, to depose or otherwise discipline, according to his desert, a member of its own body, and to reinstate a minister whom it has suspended or deposed, when trustworthy evidence of repentance and reformation appears.

The Classis shall give necessary attention to the education of pious men for the Gospel ministry, and to the cause of missions; it shall diligently prosecute the work of missions through its Permanent Home Missions Committee, whose rules and procedures shall not conflict with those of

Synod.

ARTICLE 83. Classis shall have access to all congregational records, according to the provisions of Articles 66 and 75 of this Constitution, and shall hear and decide all cases of reference, complaint and appeal, as well as all questions respecting ministers or their congregation which may arise within its jurisdiction and are regularly brought before it, such as organizing new congregations, determining boundaries of congregations and charges, deciding controversies between congregations or charges, forming, reconstructing, or dissolving charges, as may be requested or as Classis may deem expedient. Classis, however, shall exercise its right of dividing or reconstructing a charge or charges only after having counseled with the Consistories or Joint Consistories of the charges involved, and such action shall require a two-thirds vote of Classis.

ARTICLE 84. An ordained minister or a licentiate shall not be received by Classis until he has presented a regular certificate of dismission from the Classis to which he belongs. The reception of a minister from another denomination shall not be final until it is confirmed by Synod.

ARTICLE 85. An ordained minister or a licentiate shall be amenable to the Classis that dismissed him and his name shall be retained on its roll until he shall have been received by the Classis to which he has been dismissed. The dismission of an ordained minister at once annuls any previous appointment or election of him, by Classis, as a member of a committee, or as a delegate to Synod.

ARTICLE 86. A Classis dismissing an ordained minister or a licentiate shall specify in its minutes the particular Classis or other denomination to which he is dismissed; and in receiving a minister or a licentiate, it shall in like manner specify the particular Classis or other denomination from which he has been received. A certificate of dismission shall be valid for only one year from its date.

ARTICLE 87. A Classis shall not refuse to receive an ordained minister or a licentiate dismissed to it by another Classis unless there are manifest grounds of objection against his doctrine or morals, in which case the certificate of dismission shall be returned to the Classis, with a specific statement of the grounds of objection; whereupon, the Classis shall take these objections into consideration, and if it finds no sufficient reason to change its action the whole question shall be referred to Synod for decision. When an ordained minister or a licentiate is received by any Classis, it shall at once give official notice of his reception to the Classis that dismissed him.

ARTICLE 88. Whenever a minister or a licentiate willfully neglects to attend the annual meetings of his Classis and fails to report to it, he renders himself liable to suspension from office; and Classis shall at once cite him to trial and proceed in his case according to the Constitution of the Church. This article does not apply to honorably retired ministers.

ARTICLE 89. A Classis at its first meeting after the Minutes of the Synod have been distributed, shall take action on all matters referred; and also on all ordinances and constitutional amendments approved by the Synod and sent down to the Classis for ratification or rejection; and shall report its action to the next stated meeting of the Synod.

ARTICLE 90. A special meeting of Classis may be called at any time by the President; and at the written request of three ministers and three delegate elders, specifying the particular business to be transacted, he shall call such a meeting. The party or parties, for whose benefit it is called, as determined by the Executive Committee prior to the call, shall pay the expenses incurred. At least two weeks before the time of such meeting the Stated Clerk shall notify the members by circular of the time and place of meeting, and the items of business properly before the body. In case of the death or removal of the President, or if the business to be transacted implicates him, the power of calling the meeting is vested in the Stated Clerk. If either of these contingencies should exist with respect to the Stated Clerk also, two ministers and two elders, members of the Classis, may call the meeting.

ARTICLE 91. A Classis at its spring meeting shall appoint its President, Stated Clerk and one other of its members an Executive Committee, of which the President shall be chairman. This Committee shall represent Classis during the interval between meetings; and in all cases when between the parties concerned there is no question at issue, and in which at least two weeks notice of the proposed action has been given in writing by the President to every member of Classis and written objection to said action has not been made to any member of the committee nor a special meeting of Classis demanded; the Committee shall have power to dissolve a pastoral relation, to dismiss or receive a minister or a licentiate, to confirm a call, to appoint a committee to ordain a licentiate and install a pastor; to permit a minister or a licentiate to minister as a regular supply of vacant congregations, and to authorize the organization of new congregations. It shall also be the duty of this Committee to counsel with and advise the Consistory and Spiritual Council of a vacant charge, to aid the Consistory in securing a pastor, and to assist a minister in obtaining a suitable field of labor. This Committee shall also serve as advisors in the amicable adjustment of disputes in the administration of the affairs of the congregations or charges. The Committee shall, at the close of the year, present a full report of its acts and proceedings to Classis for information and incorporation in its minutes. Classis shall pay the necessary expenses of this Committee.

ARTICLE 92. The Stated Clerk shall have charge of the books and papers of Classis, and shall issue all its official documents, signed by himself and the President, with the seal of Classis affixed. At least thirty days before the annual meeting of Classis he shall furnish every pastor with a copy of the blank form of the statistical report. He shall transmit to Synod at its annual meeting a certain copy of the minutes of all the meetings of Classis held during the year, in the form and order required by the rules of Synod. He shall furnish pastoral charges and individuals with a certified copy of any proceedings in which they are specially concerned. If Synod meets as a delegated body, he shall before its annual meeting furnish the Stated Clerk with credentials of the delegates, primarii and secundi, elected to represent Classis.

ARTICLE 93. On the dissolution of a Classis, the Synod shall have jurisdiction over its members and congregations, and shall transfer them to another Classis or other Classes. It shall have charge and control of the property of said dissolved Classis, if such charge and control does not conflict with the civil law, and shall determine any case of discipline begun by the Classis and not concluded.

ARTICLE 94. The Classes, through their respective Stated Clerks, shall make report at least annually to the Stated Clerk of the Synod of all licensures, ordinations, suspensions, depositions, dismissions, or erasures of names of ministers, together with the time and place; and in the case of the decease of a licentiate or a minister, his name and the time and place of decease.

SECTION 5

The Synod

ARTICLE 95. The Synod is composed of at least four Classes and represents the whole Church. It is the highest judicatory and the last resort in all cases respecting the government of the Church. It shall meet annually, either in general convention or as a delegated body. In general convention it consists of all the ministers and one elder from each pastoral charge of the Classes constituting the Synod; as a delegated body it consists of the ministers and elders chosen by its Classes according to a basis of representation adopted by itself with the concurrence of at least two-thirds of its Classes. A suspended minister shall not be counted in the basis of representation to Synod. Its title shall be: THE SYNOD OF THE REFORMED CHURCH IN THE UNITED STATES.

ARTICLE 96. Any number of members convened at the time and place appointed for a meeting, in which a majority of the Classes is represented, shall constitute a quorum, which quorum shall contain not fewer than one minister and one elder from each of the Classes necessary to a majority of the Classes. At least one-third of the delegates shall be elders.

ARTICLE 97. The annual sessions shall be opened with religious services, including the preaching of a sermon by the President, or by some other member designated by him or by the Synod, after which the organization shall be effected and the business shall proceed according to the Rules of Order prescribed by the Synod.

ARTICLE 98. The Synod shall annually review the proceedings of its Classes. The report of the standing Committee on the Minutes of Classes shall embrace the following topics:

1. Procedures with respect to the Constitution and Church order.

2. Requests and references from Classes to the Synod.

3. Complaints and appeals to the Synod.

4. Decisions of the Classes on subjects referred to them by the Synod.

5. Licensures; ordinations; ordained ministers received, dismissed, deceased, suspended or deposed; licentiates received or dismissed, and licenses revoked.

6. Time and place of next annual meeting of each Classis, with the names and post office addresses of its President, Stated Clerk and Treasurer.

ARTICLE 99. The actions of the Classes upon an ordinance or an amendment of the Constitution of the Church shall be incorporated in regular order in the minutes of the Synod.

ARTICLE 100. The Synod has power to hear and determine complaints and appeals, and for this purpose may appoint a Judicial Committee which shall consist of three ministers and two elder delegates to the Synod.

All complaints and appeals not involving charges of errors in fundamental Christian doctrines, when brought before the Synod, may be referred to this Committee.

The Committee shall meet during the session of the Synod to hear appeals or complaints referred, and shall determine, under the provision of the Constitution, the regularity and irregularity of all papers, and consider the questions or qualities at issue, and then by a majority shall come to a decision in the case. It shall bring a report of its findings, giving a succinct statement of the main issue. If the Synod by a majority vote approves the report, it shall stand as the final decision of the Synod.

The Synod has power to give advice in a case referred to it by a Classis, to establish new Classes within its own limits, and to determine all controversies between Classes and between ministers or congregations of different Classes. A Classis, however, cannot be dissolved, nor can any part of it be united with another Classis without its own consent.

ARTICLE 101. The Synod shall give necessary attention to the education of pious men for the Gospel ministry, and to the cause of missions both in the home and in the foreign field. Its missionary operations shall be under the authority and control of the Synod.

The Synod shall diligently prosecute the work of Home Missions, of Foreign Missions, of Christian Education, and of Ministerial Relief by committees, which are to be elected and governed in their proceedings by rules established by the Synod. At the annual meeting of the Synod each committee shall submit a report of its operations and a statement of its present condition.

ARTICLE 102. The Synod may establish and maintain a Committee of Publication, whose particular purpose shall be the publication and sale of such church papers and books as are adapted to promote sound knowledge and true religion. At every annual meeting of the Synod, the Committee shall submit for examination and review a full statement of its operations during the year and of its present condition.

ARTICLE 103. The Synod shall prepare the following forms: constitution for a congregation; constitution for a joint consistory; certificate of licensure; testimonial of ordinations; certificate of dismission of a minister; call to a minister; call to a teacher of theology; certificate of dismission of a church member; statistical report of a pastoral charge; statistical report of a Classis; statistical report of the Synod; church register; accusations; citation of an accused person; citation of a witness; form for qualifying a witness; order of business and rules of order for the Classes and the Synod. These forms may be changed or amended at any stated meeting of the Synod by a two-thirds vote.

ARTICLE 104. All proposed ordinances of the Church, such as a constitution, a catechism, a hymn book and a liturgy, as well as all amendments of ordinances, must first be approved by a two-thirds vote of the

Synod at a stated meeting, and then be submitted to all the Classes for ratification or rejection. If at the next stated meeting of the Synod it shall appear that more than one-third of the Classes have rejected the ordinance or amendment, the same is rejected and shall be so declared by the Synod; otherwise it shall be declared adopted and be binding on the whole Church.

ARTICLE 105. The original records of all proceedings of the Synod and all documents, letters and papers having reference to its proceedings, shall be carefully preserved by the Stated Clerk and deposited in such place as the Synod shall direct; and a document or paper shall not be removed by any person whatever without permission obtained from the Synod, or, during its recess, from the Stated Clerk.

ARTICLE 106. At least forty days before the regular meeting of the Synod, its Stated Clerk shall furnish the Stated Clerks of the several Classes with the blank forms of the credentials for delegates to Synod.

ARTICLE 107. A special meeting of Synod shall be called by the President, or, in case of his death or removal, by the Stated Clerk, whenever six ministers and four elders, members of the Synod, request it in a written communication specifying the particular business to be transacted. At least three weeks before the Synod convenes the Stated Clerk shall notify the members by circular of the time and place of meeting, and the items of business properly before the body.

ARTICLE 108. All credentials, calls to Teachers of Theology and agreements to which Synod is a party, shall be signed by the President and the Stated Clerk, and shall have the seal of Synod attached. The Stated Clerk shall attest all extracts from the records of Synod, and shall have charge of all the records and papers, and of the seal of Synod.

ARTICLE 109. The Stated Clerk of the Synod shall provide and accurately keep a Register of Licensures and Ordinations of ministers throughout the Church, said Register showing the full name of the licentiate or ordained minister, with the date of licensure or ordination, or both, the name of the Classis by which the minister was licensed or ordained, and the time and place of licensure or ordination, the time and place of the minister's decease, with sufficient space for memoranda of the facts in case of the dismission of the minister to another Church, or of erasure of his name in the case of a transfer of his church relationship without dismission, or in case of his suspension or deposition from the ministry. The Register shall have an alphabetical index.

ARTICLE 110. The Synod shall have power to maintain correspondence with Churches with which it has fraternal relations.

ARTICLE 111. The Synod at its regular meeting shall elect a President, a Vice President, a Stated Clerk, and a Treasurer.

The Executive Committee of Synod shall consist of the President, the Vice President, the Stated Clerk, and two other delegates. At least two members of the Committee shall be elders. The Committee shall meet at least once between the annual meetings of Synod and also at the call of the Chairman or three members of the Committee.

The Executive Committee shall aid in stimulating the spiritual life of the Church by coordinating the work of the Committees of the Synod; preparing the order of business for the meetings of Synod, and, with the pastor loci, preparing the program of the Synod meetings. In the interim between meetings of Synod, proposed actions regarding the administration of the business of Synod shall be given in writing by the President to all the members of the Synod and shall be implemented unless written objection is received within thirty days from at least two members of Synod who are from different Classes. The duties of the Executive Committee shall be subject to revision at each session of the Synod. A record of the Executive Committee proceedings shall be kept and submitted to the Synod. The President of the Executive Committee of Synod shall annually submit a report to the Synod on the state of the Church, making use of the reports of the Presidents of the Executive Committees of the Classes.

PART III DISCIPLINE

SECTION 1

Discipline in General

ARTICLE 112. Christian discipline is the exercise of that authority and the application of those laws which the Lord Jesus Christ has established in His Church, to preserve its purity and honor, and to promote the spiritual welfare of its members.

ARTICLE 113. An offense is anything in doctrine, principles, or practice of a church member, officer, or judicatory that is contrary to the Word of God: and nothing shall be admitted as matter of accusation or considered an offense which cannot be proved contrary to the Scriptures or to the regulations of the Church founded on them. The following sins especially merit discipline: heresy, schism, blasphemy, adultery, fornication, lascivious wantonness, theft, fraud, perjury, lying, contentiousness, intemperance, profanation of the Lord's Day, impudent scoffing, cruelty, and other violations of the Ten Commandments.

ARTICLE 114. Discipline shall be exercised in the form of admonition, censure, erasure of name, suspension, deposition, excommunication and restoration. The Spiritual Council shall inform the disciplined offender(s) of the right to appeal, the right to counsel, and the necessary procedures in filing an appeal.

ARTICLE 115. Should any of the lower judicatories pass an action of censure or reproof upon an individual or any part in the Church in their unavoidable absence, the Secretary or Stated Clerk of said judicatory shall give those concerned immediate notice of such action; and should they feel aggrieved by it, they shall have thirty days time from date of notice for giving notice of appeal to the officers of said judicatory, and thirty days further time for lodging their reasons for appeal.

ARTICLE 116. Every case in which there is a charge of offense against a church member or officer shall be known, in its original and appellate stages, as a judicial case. Every other case shall be known as a nonjudicial or administrative case.

SECTION 2

Members – Unconfirmed and Confirmed

ARTICLE 117. All members of the Church are subject to its government and discipline. If the unconfirmed fall into sinful ways, the pastor and elders shall remind the parents of their duty in regard to them, and shall also seek by direct approach to bring them to the obedience of Christ.

ARTICLE 118. Members of the Church who upon being convicted of an offense reject the admonition of the Spiritual Council or judicatory that found them guilty, or who have committed an act of public scandal, shall be suspended from the communion of the Church. Those thus suspended shall be treated not as enemies, but as erring brethren, and shall be admonished as such, in accordance with apostolic direction (2 Thess. 3:6œ15). But if this suspension and these admonitions are ineffectual, offenders shall be excommunicated (Matt. 18:17). A suspension may or may not be announced publicly, at the discretion of the Church judicatory that tried the case; a sentence of excommunication, however, shall always be publicly pronounced.

ARTICLE 119. If a member is negligent in partaking of the Holy Communion, or refuses to contribute to the support of the Church, or continually absents himself from public worship, such conduct, in one or all of these requirements, shall be regarded as an offense against the Church, and he shall be admonished by the pastor or elders. If after admonition he continues in such negligence of duty, the Spiritual Council shall notify him that he is no longer in good and regular standing. If after not less than six months and not more than one year of such suspension he continues in such neglect of duty, the Spiritual Council shall erase his name.

If any member shall unite with another congregation of the Reformed Church or of another denomination without a certificate of dismission, the Spiritual Council shall likewise erase his name.

When a member is erased, it shall be specified in the minutes of the Spiritual Council whether this action is administrative or judicial.

SECTION 3

Ministers, Elders and Deacons

ARTICLE 120. If a minister, an elder or a deacon shall commit an offense that brings dishonor upon the Church or is punishable in the criminal courts, such a person shall upon trial and conviction by a church judicatory be removed from office; if an elder or a deacon, by the Spiritual Council; if a minister, by his Classis. In case a minister is involved in a grave public scandal, the Spiritual Council shall temporarily prevent him from exercising his ministerial function and refer him at once to his Classis for trial.

ARTICLE 121. If an ill report concerning the moral conduct of a minister, an elder or a deacon is in circulation, the Spiritual Council shall institute an immediate investigation and proceed as the interests of religion and as justice to the individual may require. If the Spiritual Council neglects to investigate ill reports concerning a minister, the Classis shall investigate them without waiting to be requested by the Spiritual Council. But if the Classis discovers that the Spiritual Council is already occupied with the case, it shall for a reasonable time await the result of the inquiry. A prosecution based on evil rumors shall not be instituted unless there is a specification of particular sin or sins and the rumors are generally circulated, permanent and not transient, and accompanied with strong presumption of truth (1 Tim. 5:19).

ARTICLE 122. If a pastor shall have been suspended or deposed from his ministerial office, the relation previously existing between him and his pastoral charge shall be dissolved and the charge declared vacant.

ARTICLE 123. If a minister accused of an offense shall refuse to appear, either in person or by counsel, after having been cited twice, he shall for his contumacy be suspended from his office; and if after another citation he refuses to appear, either in person or by counsel, he shall be suspended from the communion of the Church, if the alleged offense warrants such suspension.

ARTICLE 124. An accusation in case of scandal shall not be heard unless presented within one year after the crime is alleged to have been committed, except it can be shown that insurmountable difficulties existed, which prevented the presentation of the accusation within that time.

SECTION 4

Parties in Cases of Process

ARTICLE 125. Judicial proceedings against alleged offenders shall be instituted only on accusation by a communicant member or by a judicatory finding it necessary to investigate an offense.

ARTICLE 126. When an individual brings an accusation, he is named as the accuser; and when an accusation is brought by a judicatory of the Church, "The Reformed Church in the United States" shall be named as accuser. The person or persons against whom the accusation is brought shall be named as the accused.

ARTICLE 127. When an accusation has been brought by a judicatory, it shall appoint a committee of one or more of its members to conduct the proceeding in all its stages until the final issue is reached; but the judicatory which appointed the committee of counsel may change it, and may also appoint assistant counsel in the case at any stage of the proceeding, the same privilege either of engaging other counsel or of engaging assistant counsel being accorded to the accused.

ARTICLE 128. In cases of alleged personal injuries, a proceeding shall not be allowed unless those means for reconciliation have been tried and have failed which are required by our Lord (Matt. 18:15œ17).

SECTION 5

Charges and Specifications

ARTICLE 129. The charge or charges shall be in writing and shall set forth the alleged offense, and the specifications shall set forth the facts relied upon to sustain the charge or charges. Each offense shall be set forth as a separate charge; and each specification shall declare, as far as possible, the time, place and circumstances of the offense, and shall be accompanied with the names of the witnesses.

SECTION 6

Process and Trial

ARTICLE 130. When charges are made that an offense has been committed, they must be filed with the Stated Clerk or Secretary of the judicatory to which they are directed, who shall give one copy to the accuser and one to the accused. The Stated Clerk or Secretary shall immediately inform the President of the judicatory of the filing of the charges or accusations.

ARTICLE 131. If charges are made against the Stated Clerk or Secretary of the judicatory, they shall be filed with the presiding officer, and he shall proceed to perform the duties of the Stated Clerk or Secretary in the matter until another Stated Clerk or Secretary shall have been appointed for the occasion; and if they are made against the presiding officer, the Secretary or Stated Clerk shall proceed to perform the duties of the presiding officer in the matter until the judicatory can meet and appoint a presiding officer for the occasion.

ARTICLE 132. The President of the judiciary in which the charges have been filed, or in case of his disqualification the Stated Clerk or Secretary, shall call a meeting for the hearing of the case, in the manner and form in which such judiciary is usually called for the transaction of business. The Secretary or Stated Clerk, or in case of his disqualification the President, shall issue a citation according to the form prescribed by the Synod. Such citation and one of the copies of the charges, with the names of witnesses, shall be served on the accused at least thirty days before the trial, in person if possible, otherwise either by leaving them at his last known place of residence with an adult member of his family or household, or by mailing them in a certified letter with return receipt requested. The accuser also shall be notified of the time and place of the trial by the Stated Clerk or Secretary, or in the case of his disqualification by the President, at least ten days previous to the trial.

ARTICLE 133. If the accused refuses to obey the citation, he shall be cited a second time to appear at such time as the judiciary may deem reasonable, but not within less than ten days. If he still refuses to appear, not only shall he be liable for censure for contumacy, but the judiciary may proceed with the investigation and decision of the case as if he were present, in which case the judiciary shall appoint some person or persons to represent him as counsel.

ARTICLE 134. The President, or the Stated Clerk or Secretary of the judiciary which is to hear the case shall, when requested, issue citation to the witness or witnesses according to the form prescribed by the Synod.

Such citation shall be served upon each witness in like manner as provided in Article 132 for service of citation upon the accused. A person disobeying a citation thus issued and served is guilty of disobedience and contempt, and may for such offense be suspended (if a member of the Church) from the rights and privileges of the Church, or be reprimanded by the judiciary.

ARTICLE 135. The testimony of witnesses who, on account of distance, ill health, or other unavoidable circumstances, cannot appear at the trial of a case, may be taken by either party before a notary public or a justice of the peace, or before a member of the Church designated as a commissioner by the judiciary, provided the part in whose interest the testimony is taken notifies the opposite party, at least ten days previously, when and where the testimony is to be given, and what it is expected to prove. The opposite party may be present and cross-examine the witness, or may send questions for such cross-examination. The testimony thus taken may be read at any and all stages of the trial, provided the notary or justice or commissioner has certified thereto that said witnesses were duly qualified, and that the testimony is their testimony and was reduced to writing by him and was taken at the time and place specified in the notice.

ARTICLE 136. Trials shall be conducted in open or closed session, as the majority of the judicatory may determine. Trials for heresy shall be conducted in open session.

ARTICLE 137. An accuser may be represented by counsel, but only ministers and elders of the Reformed Church in the United States, in good and regular standing, shall appear as counsel in a judicatory.

ARTICLE 138. Exceptions to the jurisdiction of the judicatory, to the regularity of its organization, to the sufficiency of the charges and specifications, must be made at the meeting named in the citations, either before or after the charges are made. The judicatory shall determine all such preliminary objections, and may dismiss the case, or, in the furtherance of justice, may permit amendments to the specifications or charges which do not change their nature.

ARTICLE 139. If the proceedings are found in order and the charges and specifications are considered sufficient to put the accused on his defense, and there is not an acknowledgment of guilt, the trial shall proceed; but if the guilt is acknowledged, the judicatory shall pronounce sentence without further process of trial.

ARTICLE 140. The witnesses, after being sworn or affirmed by the President or by any member of the body whom he shall appoint, shall be examined, and, if desired, cross-examined; and other competent evidence may be presented. Questions as to order or evidence shall be decided by the President, subject to exception by either of the parties at the time the decision is rendered; and such decisions, if it is desired by either party, shall be entered upon the records of the case.

ARTICLE 141. All persons, including the accuser and the accused, are competent witnesses, except such as do not believe in the existence of God or in a future state of reward and punishment, or have not sufficient intelligence to understand the obligation of an oath. Any witness may be challenged for incompetency, and the judicatory shall decide the question.

ARTICLE 142. A member of the judicatory may be one of the witnesses in a case which comes before it. He shall be qualified as other witnesses are, and after having given his testimony may immediately resume his seat as a member of the judicatory, but shall not have a vote in the case in any of the judicatories of the Church.

ARTICLE 143. Exceptions to any of the rulings or proceedings in the trial may be taken by either of the parties, and shall be entered on the record to be available in case of an appeal.

ARTICLE 144. The charge or charges and specifications and the decision of the judicatory and the notice of appeal, if any, shall be entered on the minutes of the judicatory, all of which together with the evidence in the case duly filed and authenticated by the clerk of the judicatory shall constitute the record of the case. If demanded, copies of the record shall be promptly furnished to the parties at their expense.

ARTICLE 145. Decisions in judicial proceedings must be rendered by a majority vote of the members of the judicatory present during the entire progress of the trial. A separate vote must be taken on each charge. A sentence, however, of excommunication of a member, or of suspension or deposition of a minister, elder, or deacon from office, shall not be valid except by concurrence of two-thirds of the members voting. The decision and the sentence shall be publicly pronounced by the President in the judicatory at the conclusion of the proceedings. Motion for a new trial or for a mitigation of sentence shall be heard and decided immediately after the conclusion of the trial. Decisions, sentence, exceptions, motions and further proceedings on them, and notice of appeal shall be duly recorded in the minutes of the trial in the order in which they occur.

SECTION 7

References

ARTICLE 146. A reference is a submission of a pending matter by a lower to the next higher judicatory and may be made either for advice or for ultimate decision by such higher judicatory.

ARTICLE 147. In matters of reference members of the lower judicatory may vote in the higher judicatory.

ARTICLE 148. A judicatory may refuse to give final judgment in a matter of reference, and may remit the whole case either with or without advice to the lower judicatory.

ARTICLE 149. In all cases of reference the record of the proceedings in the lower judicatory shall be transmitted to the higher judicatory, and the judicatory to which a reference is made shall determine the method of procedure to be adopted for hearing and disposing of such reference.

SECTION 8

Complaints

ARTICLE 150. A complaint is a written representation made for grievances other than those that necessitate an accusation and a judicial trial. Any member of the Church in good and regular standing shall have the right of complaint, provided that due notice is given to the party against whom complaint is made.

ARTICLE 151. If the constitutional requirements for the regularity of a complaint have been met, the judicatory to which the complaint has been made shall declare it in order; and all complaints shall be so disposed of by the judicatory to which they are made that a just, correct and intelligent conclusion may be reached.

ARTICLE 152. If the official act or decision of an officer of the Church is the ground of complaint, the complaint shall be brought before the judicatory in whose name or by whose authority he acted. The complaint shall be lodged by the complainant with the Stated Clerk or Secretary of the judicatory, a copy shall be served by the Stated Clerk or Secretary on the officer complained against at least ten days before the complaint is heard.

ARTICLE 153. If the official decision of a church judicatory is complained of, the complaint shall be brought before the next higher judicatory. Immediate notice of complaint shall be given, and shall be recorded by the Stated Clerk or Secretary, and the President shall at once appoint a committee to defend the action of the judicatory before the next higher tribunal. The complaint and of the reasons for it must be filed by the complainant with the Stated Clerk or Secretary of the body complained of within thirty days after the final adjournment of the body. If reasons of complaint shall have been filed with the Stated Clerk or Secretary within the prescribed time, he shall at once inform the chairman of the committee appointed to defend the judicatory, and furnish him with a copy of the complaint and the reasons for it. Notice of complaint, together with the complaint and the reasons for it, filed with the Stated Clerk or Secretary shall be certified by him to the next higher tribunal, before which at its next session such complaint shall be heard.

ARTICLE 154. Neither the complainant, nor the persons complained of, nor the members of the judicatory complained of shall vote in the case in any of the judicatories of the Church.

ARTICLE 155. Either of the parties to a complaint may complain to the next higher judicatory.

ARTICLE 156. The judiciatory against which a complaint is made shall forward its records to the higher judicatory, together with all papers relating to the matter of the complaint.

ARTICLE 157. The same method of procedure in the hearing of a complaint shall prevail as in the case of an appeal, as provided in Articles 168 and 169 of this Constitution.

ARTICLE 158. The effect of a complaint, if sustained, may be the reversal in whole or in part of the action or decision complained of. When a complaint is sustained, the lower judicatory shall be directed how to dispose of the matter.

ARTICLE 159. Whenever a complaint is entered against a decision of a judicatory by at least one-third of the members recorded as present when the decision was made, the execution of the decision shall be stayed until the final issue of the case in a higher judicatory.

SECTION 9

Appeals

ARTICLE 160. An appeal is the removal of a judicial case by a written representation from a lower to a higher judicatory, and may be taken by either of the original parties from the judgment of the lower judicatory.

ARTICLE 161. If an appeal is taken from the decision of a judicatory in a judicial case, the judicatory that rendered the decision shall defend its position in the higher judicatory by and through such representatives as it may deem proper to appoint; said representatives, however, shall be ministers or elders, or both, of the Reformed Church in the United States.

ARTICLE 162. Irregularities in the proceedings; refusal to entertain an appeal, refusal of reasonable indulgence to a party on trial; receiving improper, or declining to receive important testimony; undue haste; manifestation of prejudice in the conduct of a case; mistake or injustice in the decision or in any of the rulings of the judicatory in the matters appertaining to the case; undue severity of sentence – are good and sufficient reasons for an appeal.

ARTICLE 163. Written notice of appeal, with a copy of specifications or errors alleged, shall be given, within thirty days after the adjournment of the judicatory, to the Stated Clerk or Secretary of the judicatory appealed from, and in the case of his absence or disability or death, to the President of it, who shall file it, with the records and all papers appertaining to the case, or a certified copy of them, with the Stated Clerk of the higher judiciary, on or before the second day of its next regular meeting after the day of reception of said notice, and shall furnish the chairman of the committee appointed to defend the judiciary with a copy of the specifications of errors alleged.

ARTICLE 164. The appellant shall appear, in person or by counsel, before the judiciary appealed to, at or before the close of the second day's session of its next stated meeting after the date of filing of the notice of appeal, prepared to proceed with the appeal. If the appellant does not appear before the judiciary appealed to, and fails to show, to the satisfaction of the judiciary, that said appellant was unavoidably prevented from so doing, the appeal shall be considered abandoned, and the judgment of the lower judiciary shall stand. The judiciary appealed to shall proceed to hear an appeal whether the judiciary appealed from appears or not, unless it is shown that notice of appeal was not properly served on the judiciary appealed from.

ARTICLE 165. All cases of appeal of which the records and papers, or certified copies of them, have been placed in the hands of the Stated Clerk of the judiciary appealed to, shall be called up by him as soon as possible after the permanent organization of the judiciary; he shall state the names of the original parties, read the accusation and decision and sentence, state the name of the judiciary appealed from and the names of the appellants, and read the reasons filed for the appeal.

ARTICLE 166. In case the Stated Clerk or Secretary of the lower judiciary has failed to file the records of an appeal as provided in Article 163, he shall be referred to his judiciary to be dealt with as the case may require; and the appellant or the judiciary appealed from may furnish a copy of said records, and, provided both shall agree as to its correctness, the same shall be taken as if it had been filed by the Stated Clerk or Secretary.

ARTICLE 167. Testimony that has not been brought before the lower judiciary shall not be admitted in the higher, except by consent of both parties. If new evidence arises which is likely to alter the aspect of the case materially, the case must be sent back to the lower judiciary for a new investigation.

ARTICLE 168. After an appeal shall have been called up and stated by the clerk, the presiding officer shall appoint a committee whose duty it shall be to take charge of all the records and papers in the case, examine the same thoroughly, and report on them:

1. Whether or not the appeal is regular and ready for hearing.

2. Propose to the judicatory the day and hour the appeal shall be heard.

3. The time to be granted to each party to present the case.

ARTICLE 169. When the time appointed for the hearing of an appeal arrives, it shall have precedence over all other business and shall be heard as follows:

1. The papers and records in the case shall be read in proper order, except such parts as may be omitted by consent.

2. The parties shall be heard, the appellant opening and closing.

3. Opportunity shall be given to the members of the judicatory appealed from to be heard.

4. Opportunity shall be given to the members of the higher judicatory to be heard.

5. The vote shall then be taken, without further debate, separately on each specification, the question being put in the form: Shall the specification be sustained? The specification having been read by the clerk and the question put by the President, the roll shall be called and the vote be taken. If not one of the specifications shall be sustained and no error be found, the judgment of the lower judicatory shall stand. If an error or errors shall be found, the judicatory appealed to shall determine whether the judgment of the lower judicatory shall be reversed or modified; or the case remanded for a new trial; and the decision, accompanied with a recital of the error or errors found, shall be entered on the record. If the judicatory deems it wise, a definition of its action may be adopted, which shall be a part of the record of the case.

ARTICLE 170. Neither the appellant nor the members of the judicatory appealed from shall vote in the case in any judicatories of the Church.

ARTICLE 171. The necessary effect of an appeal is to stay all further proceedings in the case of admonition, of censure, or of erasure of name; but in the case of suspension, or of deposition, or of excommunication, the judgment shall remain in force until finally reversed.

ARTICLE 172. The decisions of the last judicatory to which an appeal has been taken shall be valid and binding.

SECTION 10

Judicial Committee

Refer to Article 100.

SECTION 11

Restoration

ARTICLE 173. Members of the Church, deacons, elders, licentiates, or ministers who are under discipline may be reinstated either by the judicatory which disciplines them, or, with its official consent, by a co-ordinate judicatory; provided, however, that the evidence of their repentance and amendment is satisfactory. The reinstatement of a minister shall not be final until it shall have been approved by the Synod.

ARTICLE 174. A minister or a licentiate who has been deposed for the sin of adultery or of fornication, or for any offense that affixes a public scandal to his character, shall not be restored to the ministry unless it shall clearly appear to the judicatory which deposed him that the restoration can be effected without injury to the cause of religion.

ARTICLE 175. If a minister shall have been deposed but not excommunicated, he shall be entitled to the rights of a communicant member; and Classis shall furnish him with a certificate to any congregation with which he may desire to connect himself. Such certificate shall state his exact relation to the Church.

PART IV DOCTRINE AND WORSHIP

SECTION 1

Doctrine

ARTICLE 176. The Holy Scriptures of the Old and New Testaments, which are called canonical, being recognized as genuine and inspired, are received as the true and proper Word of God, infallible and inerrant, and the ultimate rule and measure of the whole Christian faith and doctrine.

ARTICLE 177. The Heidelberg Catechism, the Belgic Confession of Faith, and the Canons of Dort are received as authoritative expressions of the truths taught in the Holy Scriptures, and are acknowledged to be the subordinate standards of doctrine in the Reformed Church in the United States.

SECTION 2

Worship

ARTICLE 178. The essential parts of public worship are a call to worship, salutation, invocation, singing, prayer, reading of the Word, preaching a sermon, giving the offerings, the benediction, and the doxology. These elements of worship approved or recommended by the Synod shall be used in the regular Lord's Day service.

ARTICLE 179. Christmas, Good Friday, Easter, Ascension, Pentecost – and all days appointed by ecclesiastical or civil authority for fasting or thanksgiving – may be duly respected and observed by congregations and families by attending public worship in their churches.

ARTICLE 180. The Lord's Day (Sunday) shall be kept a holy day, devoted to the public worship of the Lord, to reading the Holy Scriptures, to private devotions, and to works of love and mercy. Weekday meetings for prayer and daily family worship are also commended as important religious services.

SECTION 3

The Sacraments

ARTICLE 181. The sacraments of the Church instituted by Christ are two: Holy Baptism and the Lord's Supper.

ARTICLE 182. Children are received into the Church by baptism and are subject to its care and discipline. As soon as they are old enough to learn the Catechism and to be benefited by the pastor's instruction, they shall become members of the catechetical class.

ARTICLE 183. A child shall be baptized if one of its parents is a member of the Church.

ARTICLE 184. The previous article shall not be so construed as to prevent persons who adopt orphans or other children into their families from bringing them to God for baptism and giving them the sign and seal of the covenant of grace.

ARTICLE 185. Adults shall be baptized if a minister has ascertained that they possess correct views of Christian doctrine, give evidence of true repentance and faith, and are willing to yield obedience to the requirements of Christ. But if in these respects the minister discovers deficiencies, he shall direct them to attend the usual catechetical instruction, and shall afterward proceed in relation to them as with other catechumens. If this, however, is impractical, he shall instruct them in some other suitable way.

ARTICLE 186. Baptism shall be administered publicly in the Church, if possible. The forms provided in the liturgy of the Reformed Church in the United States shall be used.

ARTICLE 187. The sacrament of the Lord's Supper shall be observed publicly in every congregation at least twice a year, and the celebration conducted according to the established order of the Reformed Church in the United States.

ARTICLE 188. Every sermon based upon Scripture must necessarily conform to the spiritual meaning of the Lord's Supper; and unless the Spiritual Council has taken official disciplinary measures against a communicant member, he shall not be denied the privileges of attending the Lord's Table. In the congregational records the dates on which the Holy Communion has been administered and the names of the members who have communed shall be noted.

ARTICLE 189. Members, in good standing, of other congregations of the Reformed Church, and of other denominations holding the essential doctrines of the Gospel, should be invited to participate in the observance of this sacrament.

ARTICLE 190. The Lord's Supper shall be administered to the sick and infirm communicants who are not able to come to the house of God and who express a desire to receive the sacrament.

SECTION 4

Rites

ARTICLE 191. Confirmation, ordination and marriage are sacred church rites, which shall be administered according to the order prescribed in the liturgy of the Church.

ARTICLE 192. Every pastor shall carefully prepare the youth in his pastoral charge for communicant membership in the Church by diligently instructing them in the doctrines and duties of the Christian religion. The period of instruction shall, if possible, be so extended that the pupils memorize and are able to recite the entire Heidelberg Catechism before confirmation. The course of instruction shall include catechetical explanation and memorization, Bible history, Bible readings and memorizations, and the study of the books and contents of the Bible, the Belgic Confession of Faith, the Canons of Dort, church history, also the singing and memorization of Psalms, hymns, and Scripture songs.

ARTICLE 193. Before admitting applicants for confirmation into full communion with the Church, the Spiritual Council shall be satisfied that the candidates understand the fundamental truths of the Christian religion and are governed by them in their walk and conversation.

ARTICLE 194. In the act of ordination, whether of a minister, an elder, or a deacon, only ordained ministers and elders of the Church shall participate in the laying on of hands. A person once ordained whether as a minister of the Gospel, an elder, or a deacon, is set apart to that particular office for life, unless for sufficient reason the ordination has been revoked.

ARTICLE 195. Marriage is an ordinance of God and should be solemnized in accordance with the laws of the Church as well as the State.

ARTICLE 196. Members of the Church, having died in the faith and hope of the Gospel, shall receive a Christian burial; the burial service may be conducted according to the order prescribed by the Church.

AMENDMENTS

ARTICLE 197. This Constitution may be amended or altered in any article by a two-thirds vote of the Synod, with the concurrence of two-thirds of the Classes.

THE RULES OF ORDER OF THE

REFORMED CHURCH IN THE UNITED STATES

Table of Contents:

1. Organization

1. The president shall take the chair at the hour to which the judicatory stands adjourned or is summoned to meet, and shall immediately call the members to order and open the session with the prescribed religious services.

2. In the absence of the president the stated clerk shall call the members to order and put in nomination a president pro temp., who shall preside until the president takes his place or until an election has been held. Should the president and the stated clerk both be absent, the oldest minister in attendance shall preside.

3. The roll shall then be called, on which the names of all those entitled to a seat and having proper credentials shall have been entered and about whose right there is no contest. If a quorum is present, the judicatory shall proceed to business; but if not, any two members present may adjourn from time to time to give opportunity for a quorum to assemble.

4. If a contest is made as to the right of any one claiming a seat, or if there are present two or more sets of delegates from a lower judicatory, the matter shall at once be referred to a committee, which shall examine into the case and shall report within twenty-four hours after its appointment.

5. As soon as an organization has been fully effected an election shall be held for such officers as may be required by the Constitution of the Church or the custom of the judicatory. When two or more persons are nominated for an office, a majority of votes cast shall be required for an election.

6. Immediately after the organization the president shall define the bar of the house and no one outside of its limits shall have the privileges of a member of the judicatory.

7. A quorum to transact business in any judicatory of the Church shall consist of the number of members required by the Constitution.

II. Duties of the President

8. When the president has opened the session and found a quorum present after the first day, he shall cause the minutes of the preceding day to be read, and, if necessary, to be corrected, when he shall declare them approved; and before the final adjournment the remaining proceedings shall be read and corrected; and when no further corrections are required the president shall say: "Shall the minutes now be approved?" If no objections are made, he shall declare them to stand approved.

9. He shall preserve order, guard against a violation of the Constitution of the Church and the rules of order, and endeavor to conduct all business to a speedy and proper conclusion.

10. He shall, as soon as possible after the organization has been effected, appoint the several standing committees required for the prompt accomplishment of the

business before the judicatory; and, unless otherwise provided for, he shall appoint all special committees that may be called for in the process of business.

11. He shall keep exact account of all items of business that have been laid over or assigned to a particular day and call them up at the proper time.

12. He shall receive all minutes, reports, communications, etc., addresses to or intended for the judicatory, and with its consent refer them to the appropriate committees.

13. He shall sign the minutes and all addresses or circulars, etc., issued by the judicatory; and shall decide all questions of order subject to an appeal to the judicatory by any two members.

14. He may state a question sitting, but shall rise to put it and shall say: "As many as are in favor (as the question may be) say 'aye." After the affirmation is expressed, he shall say: "As many as are opposed say 'no." If he is in doubt as to the results or a division is called for, those voting in the affirmative shall rise, stand, and be counted; after which those voting in the negative shall also rise, stand, and be counted. The president shall then announce the result.

15. When a vote is taken by ballot in any judicatory, the president shall vote with the other members; but he shall not vote in any other case, unless the judicatory is equally divided; when, if he does not choose to vote, the question shall be lost.

III. Duties of the Stated Clerk

16. The stated clerk shall have prepared in advance of the time of the meeting of the judicatory a complete roll of its members, and, as soon as possible, perfect a roll of those members present for the use of the president. Whenever any additional members take their seats, he shall add their names, in their proper places, to the said roll.

17. He shall make correct and concise minutes of all the proceedings of the judicatory and carefully preserve them. He shall, if required, prepare a correct and authenticated copy of the minutes and transmit them in due time to the higher judicatory for review. He shall read all papers by order of the president, shall publish due notice of the time and place of all stated meetings, and, by order of the president, of all special meetings.

18. A memorial, communication, or other paper confided to his care shall not be withdrawn from the files without the warrant of the judicatory.

19. He shall make, for convenient reference, a digest of the legislative actions and of all decisions made on constitutional questions or on the rules of order by the judicatory.

IV. The Order of Business

20. After the minutes have been read and approved, an opportunity shall be given to announce in the presence of recently arrived members or of secundi in order that they may be recognized.

21. Business unfinished at a previous session shall be taken up first, unless a special order has been set for that hour.

22. Reports from permanent committees shall have precedence, unless a matter has been set for a special hour.

V. Members -- Their Rights and Duties

23. Every member shall be present within the bar of the house while the judicatory is in session, unless excused or necessarily prevented, and shall vote on each question put, unless previously excused, or unless he has a direct personal or pecuniary interest in the determination of such question.

24. Every member, in speaking, shall rise and address himself respectfully to the president, and, and having been recognized, shall proceed to address the judicatory. He shall treat the president and his fellow members with decorum and respect, shall confine himself to the subject under discussion, and shall avoid all personalities.

25. During the transaction of business, members shall not engage in private conversations; in debate they shall not address themselves to any one save the president.

26. When two or more members rise at the same time, the president shall name the one who is to speak first. A member shall not speak on the same question more than twice, no longer than one-half hour unless by consent of the body. The chairman of a committee, however, may open and close when general debate has been had on a motion reported by him. A member who has spoken on the main question may speak again on an amendment.

27. When a member, in speaking or otherwise, shall transgress the rules of order or deviate from the subject under discussion or in any way act disorderly, it shall be the privilege of any member, and the duty of the president, to call him to order. He shall take his seat immediately, unless permitted to explain, when, if the judicatory is satisfied, he may proceed to order; but if the case requires it, he shall be liable to censure or reprimand.

28. A speaker shall not be interrupted unless with his permission, or when he is out of order, or for the purpose of correcting mistakes or misrepresentations.

29. While the president is putting a question or a member is speaking, members shall not pass between the president and the speaker or walk across the floor.

30. A motion cannot be made while a member is speaking or after the president has begun to take a vote.

31. A member may change his vote before the president has announced the result, or afterward in case it does not affect the result.

VI. Committees -- Their Powers

32. The first-named member of each committee shall be the chairman. In the absence of the first-named member or in the event of his refusal to preside, the second member of the committee shall take his place; the same order of succession is to be followed as often as a vacancy occurs.

33. A committee to whom papers have been referred shall return them with its report; and a paper cannot go before a committee or become a matter for its action, unless it has been properly referred to it.

34. A majority of a committee shall constitute a quorum and it alone can make a report. A minority may submit its views in writing, or any member may submit a motion that contains a view of the minority.

35. A committee may appoint one or more sub-committees in order to facilitate its work by thus distributing it among its several members, but the final report must come from the whole committee.

36. When a special committee has made its report and it is received, the committee is by this act discharged. A report, however, *may* be recommitted; or the committee may be reappointed for another purpose.

37. A judicatory may at any time resolve itself into a committee of the whole to consider any special matter, whereupon the president shall name some one to preside, and vacate the chair. Such committee may rise at any time, after which the president shall resume the chair and the chairman of the committee shall report its action, or report progress and ask leave to sit again.

VII. Motions -- Their Precedence

38. Every motion made to a judicatory and entertained by the president shall, on the demand of any member, be reduced to writing. The president shall state the question or cause it to be read by the stated clerk before it is debated. It shall then be in possession of the house, but may be withdrawn at any time before it has been amended or a decision has been taken on it.

39. When a question is under debate, a motion shall not be entertained excepting it is one of the following motions:

- To adjourn.

- To take recess.

- To lay on the table.

- To take the previous question.

- To postpone to a certain day.

- To refer or commit.

- To amend.

- To postpone indefinitely.

These several motions shall have precedence in the order named; and a motion to refer, to postpone to a certain day, or to postpone indefinitely, having been decided, shall not be entertained again on the same day at the same state of the question.

40. If a motion under debate contains several parts, any member may request its division and a question shall be taken on each part. A motion to strike out and insert is not divisible.

41. A subject, which has been indefinitely postponed either by the operation of the previous question or by a motion for indefinite postponement or by a motion to lay on the table unconditionally, shall not again be called up during the same session of the judicatory, unless by the consent of three- fourths of the members who were present at the decision.

42. When different motions are made with respect to filling blanks, the longest time and the largest sum shall be put first

43. A motion shall not be considered as before the house unless it has been seconded and the mover recognized by the president.

VIII. Amendments

44. When a motion or proposition is under consideration, a motion to amend and a motion to amend that amendment shall be in order, and it shall also be in order to offer a further amendment in the form of a substitute for the entire proposition, and to this substitute an amendment may be offered which shall not be voted upon, however, until the original motion is perfected.

45. A motion to amend cannot be modified after the previous question has been seconded.

46. An amendment to the rules of order shall not be entertained, unless it has been seconded by a majority of the members present.

IX. Reconsideration

47. When a motion or resolution has been offered and carried or has been lost, it shall be in order for any member, who has voted with the majority, to move on the same or succeeding day a reconsideration of it. Such a motion shall take precedence of all motions, excepting the motion to adjourn or to take recess.

48. A motion to reconsider is not debatable, unless the question proposed to be reconsidered was debatable.

X. The Previous Question

49. The previous question on any motion, after a reasonable time has been allowed to discuss it, may be called. The call, to be entertained, must be made by at least one-fifth of the members present rising in their places for the purpose. The previous question shall be presented in the following form: "Shall the main question now be put?" And, until it is decided, it shall preclude all further amendments or debate on the main question. The effect of this motion, when sustained, shall be to bring the judicatory to a direct vote on all the amendments then pending, in their proper order and on the main question itself.

50. The previous question shall apply in questions of privilege as in motions generally.

XI. Questions of Privilege

51. Questions of privilege shall be:

1. Those affecting the rights of the judicatory collectively; its safety, dignity, and the integrity of its proceedings.

2. The rights, the reputation, and the conduct of the members individually in their representative capacity.

They shall have precedence of all questions except to adjourn and to take recess.

52. It shall not be a matter of privilege to have received and entered upon the minutes a protest of a member or members against the action of a judicatory.

53. The ayes and nays on any question shall be recorded when required by any member who dissents from the acts of a judicatory.

XII. Appeals

54. An appeal from the decision of the president on any point of order may be taken by any member who may briefly state the reasons for his appeal, to which the president may reply if he deems it needful. The vote shall then be taken without further debate. The form of stating the question shall be: "Shall the decision of the chair stand as the decision of this judicatory'?"

55. A question of appeal cannot be reconsidered after other business has been done.

56. An appeal is not in order while another appeal is pending.

XIII. The Motion to Lay on the Table

57. The motion to lay on the table may be made to consider more important matters, or to take up the matter at a more convenient time, or quickly to make a final disposition of it.

58. This motion shall take precedence of all other motions except the motion to adjourn, or to take recess, and shall be decided without debate.

59. All that adheres to the subject of the motion goes on the table with it except it pertains to a motion for correcting the minutes.

60. When this motion is made and lost, it cannot be made again until some change has been made in the question under consideration.

61. When a motion to lay on the table has been lost, it may be reconsidered; but when a motion to reconsider is laid on the table, that motion cannot be reconsidered.

XIV. Miscellaneous

62. The rules of order may be suspended by unanimous consent.

63. A motion to amend the rules of order shall lie over one day; and it shall require a two-third vote to carry the amendment.

64. A judicatory may sit with closed doors if, in its judgment, the matter under consideration requires it.

65. Officers, delegates to higher judicatories, members of boards, etc., shall be elected by ballot; but a judicatory may make such elections by acclamation as do not conflict with any existing law.

66. It shall be in order to take recess only when a quorum is present.

67. A motion to take recess may be offered while another question is pending, or when another member is holding the floor providing he gives his consent.

68. The motion to adjourn, to take recess, to lay on the table, or for the previous question, shall be taken without debate.

69. The ayes and nays on any question shall be recorded on the demand of any member.

70. A member shall not retire from a judicatory without the permission of the president, nor withdraw from it to return home without the consent of the judicatory.

71. Before the final adjournment of a judicatory the roll shall be called, and all members absent without permission shall be reported by the stated clerk to the body that they were sent to represent.

72. At the final adjournment, after the judicatory has united with the president in the repetition of the creed and the Lord's Prayer, he shall pronounce the apostolic benediction and declare the judicatory now adjourned to meet as ordered.

THE MODEL CONSTITUTION OF A CONGREGATION OF

THE REFORMED CHURCH IN THE UNITED STATES

Section I

Name and Object

Article 1. The name of this congregation shall be_____

Article 2. The object of this congregation shall be to provide its members with the stated preaching of the Word, the administration of the sacraments, the facilities for public worship, and the exercise of Christian discipline, and to adopt and prosecute from time to time such measures as are in harmony with the spirit, teaching and customs of the Reformed Church in the United States, and as shall tend to promote the general interests of the Redeemer's kingdom.

Article 3. This congregation shall be an organic member of the Reformed Church in the United States, and shall be governed by the constitution, laws and rules of said Church.

Section II

Officers and Their Duties

Article 4. The officers of this congregation shall be a pastor (or pastors), _____elders, _____deacons, _____trustees, a secretary, and a treasurer, whose general standard of duty shall be the Word of God and the Constitution of the Reformed Church in the United States.

Article 5. It shall be the duty of the pastor to conduct the public worship of the sanctuary, to preach the gospel, to exercise pastoral oversight of the congregation, to dispense the holy sacraments, and in conjunction with the elders to administer Christian discipline.

Article 6. It shall be the duty of the elders to watch faithfully over the spiritual interests of the congregation, to maintain order in the House of God, to aid in visiting the sick, and to contribute according to their ability to the edification and consolation of all the members. They shall also provide the elements for the Lord's Supper when requested by the pastor.

Article 7. It shall be the duty of the deacons to cooperate with the other officers of the congregation to promote its general welfare, to gather the offerings for the relief of the poor and the necessities of the congregation, to distribute the alms, and to provide for the pastor's salary under the direction of the Consistory.

Article 8. The pastor, elders and deacons of the congregation shall constitute the Consistory, which shall have oversight and government of the congregation and all the organizations. The pastor shall be the president of the Consistory, but when a charge is without a pastor, or the pastor is unable to attend, one of the elders shall be chosen to preside. A majority of the members shall constitute a quorum.

Article 9. The Consistory shall have the charge of the general affairs of the congregation, shall call congregational meetings, order collections for the apportionments of Classis and for other benevolent purposes, distribute alms through the deacons, provide for the audit of the treasurers account, and make record of its own proceedings, be the custodian of all congregational records, and submit any or all records to Classis when occasion requires it and the Classis requests it.

Article 10. The pastor or the secretary of the Consistory shall keep a complete record of all baptisms, confirmations, communicants, receptions by certificate, renewals of profession, dismissions, erasures of names, suspensions, excommunications, marriages, and deaths. These records shall be the property of the congregation.

Article 11. In calling a minister and in all matters of general interest, including the election of delegates to Classis of Synod, the Consistory shall be guided by the requirements of the Constitution of the Reformed Church in the United States.

Article 12. Unless there are difficulties, the members of the Consistory shall constitute the Trustees, who shall have the care and control of the property of the congregation as a sacred trust, whether real or personal, in accordance with the provision of the Articles of Incorporation and of the Constitution of the Reformed Church in the United States.

Article 13. The secretary of the Consistory shall also serve as the secretary of the Trustees of the congregation, and, when an elder, secretary of the Spiritual Council, and shall perform faithfully the duties generally pertaining to such office.

Article 14. The treasurer, elected by the Consistory, shall be the treasurer of the congregation, and shall keep an accurate and faithful account of all moneys received and paid out; and he shall not disburse any funds unless properly authorized. He shall submit annually a detailed report of the finances to the Consistory and to the congregation.

Article 15. The consistory shall hold stated monthly (or quarterly) meetings and may hold special meetings at such other times as may be necessary; and meet before the annual congregational meeting for the transaction of business and final settlement with the treasurer and other officers. All special meetings shall be called by the president; or, in the event of his absence, or inability or unwillingness to act, by the secretary when requested in writing to do so by a majority of the members.

Article 16. The pastor and elders shall constitute the Spiritual Council, whose duty it shall be to watch over the members of the congregation, to guard the doctrine of Christ, and to maintain strict and wholesome discipline; to admit members to full communion of the Church, and to exclude from it those who may err from the faith or offend in morals. It shall examine the catechumens applying for confirmation, and, before the observance of the Lord's Supper, inquire whether any member has departed from the doctrine of Christ in faith and practice, that those who are guilty may be disciplined as the case may require. It may furnish upon proper request members of the congregation, in good a regular standing, with certificates of dismission to another congregation in the Reformed Church in the United States or to any orthodox Protestant Church that receives members by certificate from the Reformed Church in the United States. The pastor shall be the president, but if the pastor is absent one of the elders shall be chosen to preside. A majority of the members shall constitute a quorum. It shall keep a full and accurate record of its proceedings which shall be submitted to the Classis when occasion requires it and the Classis requests it.

Section III

Elections and Organization

Article 17. Every male communicant member of the congregation, having attained the age of majority, in good and regular standing, shall be entitled to vote at all elections for pastor and officers, and on any question submitted to the congregation for action.

Article 18. An election for pastor shall be held according to the prescribed regulations of the Constitution of the Reformed Church in the United States (Art. 68).

Article 19. When a pastor shall resign his charge or when three-fourths of the members of the Consistory shall make a written request to the pastor for his resignation, the prescribed regulations of the Constitution of the Reformed Church in the United States shall be observed (Art. 19 and 30).

Article 20. An election for elders and deacons shall be held at the annual congregational meeting, and those chosen shall serve _____ years and until their successors are elected and installed. All elections for officers shall be by ballot and shall be determined by a majority of votes cast.

Article 21. Nominations for the offices of elder and deacon may be made by any member in good and regular standing to the Consistory, which shall present the name or the names of one or of two persons for each officer to be elected. Public notice of the nominations shall be given from the pulpit at least two weeks before the election. A person shall not be voted for unless regularly nominated. All nominees must be in full communion with the Church and earnestly devoted to the cause of Christ. (If possible, each congregation shall have at least two elders and two deacons.)

Article 22. Whenever a vacancy among the elders or deacons serving on the Consistory occurs by death, or resignation, or in any other way, the Consistory may fill the vacancy for the current year.

Article 23. An annual meeting of the congregation shall be held within the month of _____ for the transaction of regular business and for the election of officers. The Consistory may call a special meeting of the congregation, and at the written request of one-tenth of the communicant members shall issue a call for such meeting within two weeks after the request has been received. Two weeks' previous public notice shall be given of the time, place and purpose of a special congregational meeting. The secretary shall keep full and accurate record of the proceedings of all meetings.

Article 24. The Consistory shall elect annually two of the elders as delegates, a primarius and a secundus, to represent the charge in Classis. They shall also be the delegates to Synod whenever Synod meets in general convention. At least ten days before the annual meeting of the judicatory to which these delegates have been elected their credentials shall be sent to its Stated Clerk by the president or the secretary of the Consistory.

Section IV

Members and Their Duties

Article 25. All baptized persons shall be members of this congregation, are under its care, shall be entitled to its rights and privileges, and are subject to its government and discipline. Communicant members are those who have been duly received into its communion by confirmation, by profession of faith, by certificate, or by renewal of profession, and have not been excluded by the process of Christian discipline.

Article 26. It shall be the duty of every member of this congregation to live a sober, righteous and godly life, and to labor faithfully in bringing others unto Christ; to obey the laws and rules prescribed in the Word of God and abide by the Constitution of the Church; to contribute liberally and in proportion to his means to the support of the gospel and for the extension of the kingdom of Christ; to attend faithfully the public services of the Church, engage diligently in private devotions, and regularly partake of the Lord's Supper. Parents shall present their children at the proper time for baptism and give special attention to the Christian training of the members of their household.

Article 27. If a member is negligent in partaking of the Holy Communion or refuses to contribute to the support of the Church or continuously absents himself from the public worship, such conduct, in one or all of these requirements, shall be regarded as an offense against the Church, and he shall be admonished by the pastor or the elders. If after admonition he continues in such negligence of duty, the Spiritual Council shall notify him that he is no longer in good and regular standing. If after not less than six months and not more than one year of such suspension he continues in such neglect of duty, the Spiritual Council shall erase his name.

If any member shall unite with another congregation of the Reformed Church, or of another denomination without a certificate of dismission, the Spiritual Council shall likewise erase his name.

Article 28. Members, who, on account of change of residence or for other proper reasons, shall desire to change their membership from one congregation to another congregation of the Reformed Church in the United States or, if necessary, another orthodox Protestant Church, shall obtain a certificate of dismission and as soon as possible shall unite with the other congregation. The Spiritual Council dismissing them shall communicate immediately the fact to the Spiritual Council of the congregation to which they have been dismissed; and, when they are received, the latter shall notify promptly the former of their reception. Members dismissed shall be amenable to the congregation dismissing them until they shall have been received by another congregation. A certificate of dismission shall be valid for only one year from its date.

Section V

By-laws

Article 29. The congregation may from time to time enact such by-laws for its government as may be deemed necessary; provided, however, that they do not conflict with this constitution or the Constitution of the Reformed Church in the United States.

Section VI

Amendments

Article 30. This constitution may be altered or amended by the congregation by a vote of two-thirds of the members present either at an annual meeting or at a special meeting called for that purpose; provided that at least two weeks' notice of the proposed change shall have been given.

Made in the USA
Middletown, DE
26 December 2022